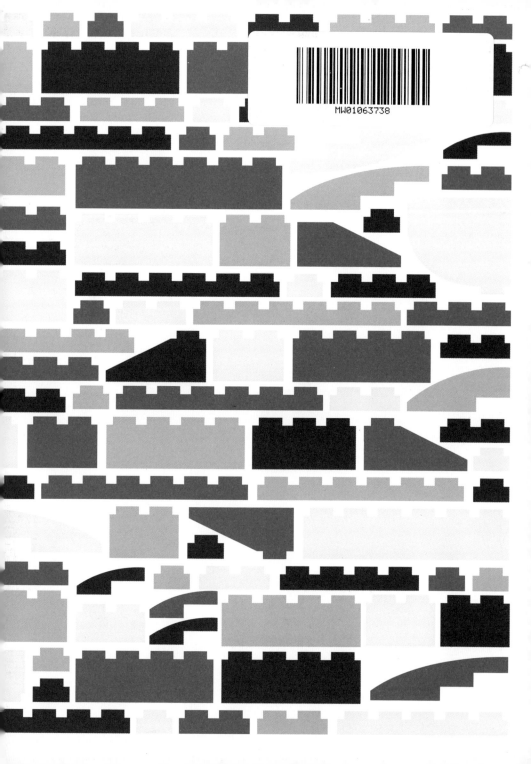

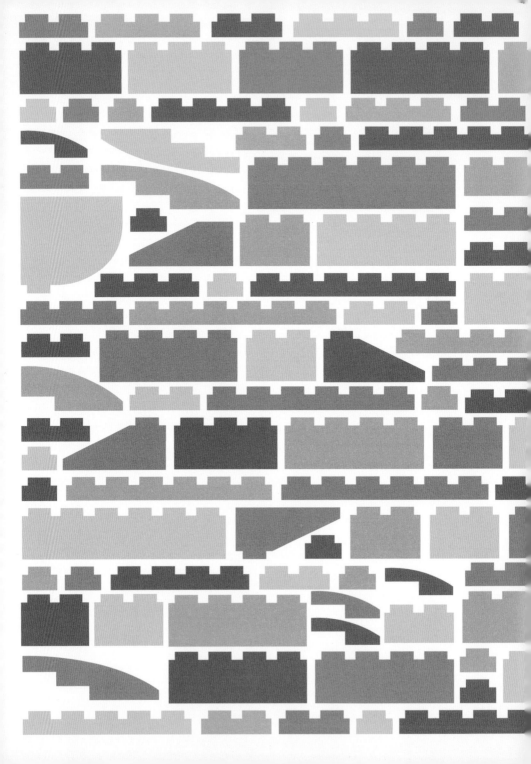

Build Every Day

Library of Congress Cataloging-in-Publication Data is available.

ISBN 978-1-7972-1413-9

Manufactured in China.

Design by MacFadden & Thorpe.

10 9 8 7 6 5 4 3 2 1

See the full range of LEGO® books and gifts at www.chroniclebooks.com.

Chronicle books and gifts are available at special quantity discounts to corporations, professional associations, literacy programs, and other organizations. For details and discount information, please contact our premiums department at corporatesales@chroniclebooks.com or at 1-800-759-0190.

Chronicle Books LLC
680 Second Street
San Francisco, California 94107
www.chroniclebooks.com

Build Every Day

Ignite Your Creativity and Find Your Flow

Alec Posta

CHRONICLE BOOKS

SAN FRANCISCO

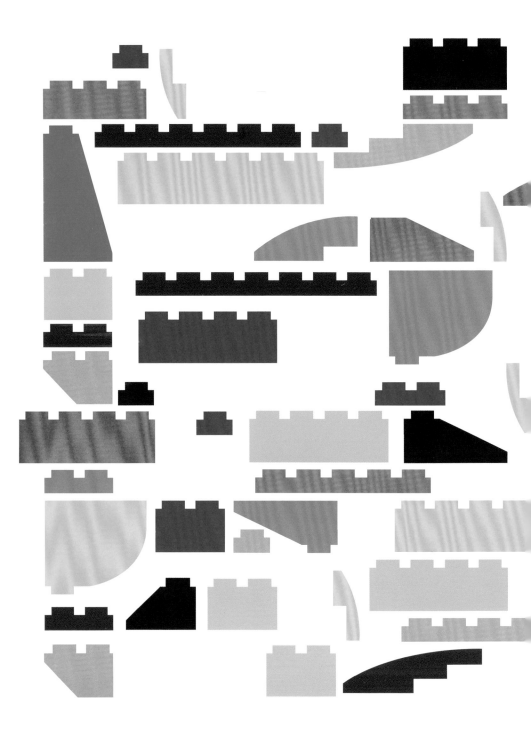

Table of Contents

Introduction

My name is Alec Posta and I am a professional LEGO® model builder. Yes: That is an actual job. For an adult. I have business cards and everything.

I work at LEGOLAND® Discovery Center Arizona where I dream up, design, and build all the custom LEGO models that go on display within our attraction. I have my own well-stocked model shop with a big window that opens out into the LEGOLAND® Park where guests can watch me work, ask me questions, and (hopefully) get inspired by my creations. I'll admit that it was pretty strange at first, working in a giant fishbowl, but nowadays I see it as one of the major perks of the job. I'm able to share my love of creativity with every person who walks up and encourage kids and adults to think beyond building instructions. What keeps me playing the whole day through is my love of the LEGO philosophy, the idea that you can create anything from just your mind and a few basic bricks.

I started building with LEGO bricks in the 1990s: an era marked by pirates, deep-sea explorers, and more transparent, fluorescent green elements than you'd ever know what to do with. My parents, being amazing and supportive as they are, encouraged me to spend my days building, drawing, finding gnarled sticks in the Arizona desert to carve into wizard staffs, and generally being creative in whatever way I saw fit. LEGO building was, of course, my medium of choice. Like most kids, I enjoyed sets. I'd circle each one I wanted in LEGO® *Club Magazine* and keep them displayed on my shelves after they were built like trophies (luckily, and maybe unsurprisingly, I didn't have a ton of trophies). As I got older, I outgrew my LEGO sets—*toys* to my teenager mind—and I turned to *cooler* pursuits, like guitar, and not caring about anything. However, the desire to create persisted.

I didn't return to LEGO building until I was (arguably) an adult in my early twenties. Coming back to it with fresh eyes helped me discover something I'd never even thought about as a child: that building can be meditative. There's a sort of Zen that comes with sitting down to create and letting time pass by as you click together brick after brick. I found myself applying lessons I'd learned from my other creative pursuits, such as music and art, to LEGO building. In the span of six years I went from "guy who played with LEGO sets as a kid" to "professional AFOL" (meaning Adult Fan of LEGO). During this process I've designed a lot, and built a lot, but I've also done a lot of *thinking* about designing and building, as well as the creative forces at work behind those concepts.

In this book I'll take you through some of these lessons as they apply to LEGO building, art, design, and beyond. The building challenges I'll put forward will require bricks, but no more than a small collection of loose parts. Embodying these ideas surely requires time, but not more than a few minutes each day. These lessons may seem small, but, like LEGO bricks, they can be built upon into a mindset that I hope will carry you through whatever challenges you come across.

Build Every Day

Today, you can build something. It can be small. It can be massive. It can be a real object or an abstract work of art. It can be colorful or minimalist, totally new, or a version of the same thing you've been working on for months. It can be weird. It can fall apart. With just a handful of bricks, you can build something, and it can change your mood, your perspective—the whole path of your day! And with some practice, it could even change the way you solve problems, in the world of building and beyond. Making time to build every day can ignite creativity, help you overcome obstacles, and find focus and flow.

Why not start right now? Go find two bricks and click them together. You've just taken the first step toward creating a new daily habit that will be both challenging and rewarding, for seasoned and novice builders alike. Then say it out loud to yourself: I'm going to build every day. Tell a fellow builder for accountability. Check off today's date in your calendar, journal, or the notes app in your phone. Today can be Day One on a journey that stretches your skills and your mind.

I do have to warn you, a daily building habit is simple to start, harder to stick with. I can hear you saying: *Impossible, Alec.*

I love building. How hard can it be? It is hard even for me. The thing about being a professional LEGO® model builder is that it's still a job, and sometimes it can really feel like one. No matter what you do for work, study at school, or even do for fun, there are days, weeks, or even whole months where you might feel uninspired. Sometimes I feel like everything I design comes up short. Creating anything feels like it takes so much *effort*. But however I may feel when I sit down to build every day, I need to open up my workshop window and try my best to design what needs to be built. For me, powering through tough times is about showing up, building a routine, and sticking to it. And (surprise, surprise) that uninspired feeling never stays forever. In fact, rising *out* of those creative slumps is often when I feel that I do my best work.

The key to doing this at home is to maintain your momentum by creating a habit. Pick a time and place, set the goal of building every day, and stick to it. With building, for example, it can be easy to hit a roadblock and put something down for days at a time if you're not feeling up to it. But this increases the risk that you'll never pick it back up. Making yourself do something every day, even on days you don't want to, is crucial when it comes to mastering a skill. If you sit down and try to design something, it doesn't turn out as expected, and you put down your bricks after five minutes—that's GREAT! You still sat down and tried: That's 100 percent better than not doing it at all.

You've already made today Day One. Commit to Day Two. I can't wait to see what you discover about bricks, building, and yourself.

....

Build It:

Commit to a week of daily building. Set aside time each day to be your building time and show up for yourself. It can be as long or as short as you like. Set a goal to work on day after day or start fresh each time you sit down. Set a timer and a build!

2 Pick a Brick and Go!

For many people, myself included, actually *starting* is the hardest part of the creative process. When it comes to designing something original, it is often difficult to match the awesomeness of what's in your head with what's being built by your hands. It's easy to *think* of a crazy, giant robot with sharks for hands, shooting ice cream out of its eyes as it walks away from an explosion, but making that idea tangible is a whole other story. When something lives only in your head, the details are allowed to be a little fuzzy. Your brain fills in all the gaps: all the structural things that aren't as cool as shark hands and dairy beams. Being forced to flesh out those gaps can lead to a sort of creative paralysis that's hard to overcome.

Luckily, there is an easy fix for this: Plan less. Let go of planning *where* or *how* to start and just dive in. In picking up your pieces and just starting, you're allowing your own skills, and the bricks that you have on hand, to guide your design process. By going in with no plan, you're not setting up any lofty expectations for how things need to look. Suddenly, the fear of failing lifts. The first brick in your masterpiece is just a brick again.

Sure, maybe you go into your building session with a broad idea but try to keep it as vague as possible. I'm going to design an animal. A building. A boat. Let the process be fluid. If you start building a dog but it's turning out too chunky and gray, make it a walrus. Now the walrus's tusks are too long? Whatever, the tusks are snakes now. Yes, you're making a walrus with snakes for tusks. That's the fun of LEGO® bricks: Once you start building you can do whatever you want!

....

Build It:

Pick a broad category: animals, plants, vehicles, buildings, people, etc. and just start building. Stop after 10 minutes and pivot to something totally new. Turn a bike into a food. A parrot into a robot.

FIND

Find Your Flow

If you've ever done something and lost track of time, you're familiar with the concept of "flow." When you allow yourself to be fully engaged in what's in front of you, so much so that every thought you have and every move you make is in service of the activity at hand, you've found your flow state.

Getting into a creative flow is something I strive to achieve every time I sit down to build, not only because it's when I do my best work, but also because it's such a joy to lose yourself in doing something you love. When I've found my flow, building with LEGO® bricks becomes meditation. All the stress in your life and any problems that have been weighing on your mind slip away and are replaced by thoughts and ideas pertaining to what you're building with your hands. Everything you think becomes much more *present*. Where is that brick? What angle should this piece be at? Does this look better in red or dark blue? These little questions that arise get your full attention and each solution carries you into the next question. Time passes unnoticed and you're fully living in the moment.

My favorite part of finding a flow, however, is that the *process* becomes the main event. When you find joy in the act of creating, the end result is less important, less significant. It becomes easy to find peace in the act of doing something you love.

. . . .

Build It:

Try building something you feel is *just* outside of your skill range. The additional challenge may help you find your flow. Let go of the end result and focus in on the click of each brick as you place it.

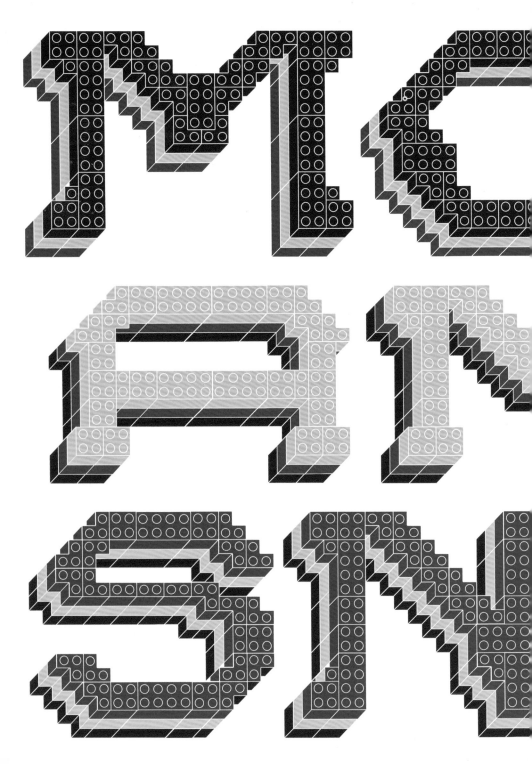

MOCs and SNOTs

As you progress as a builder, you're inevitably going to need to *talk* about the techniques and individual parts you are using in some way. Talking about the vast range of official LEGO® elements isn't always easy. With catchy, official names like *Cone 1×1 with Top Groove* and *Bar 1×8 with Brick 1×2 Curved Top End,* it's no wonder that builders of all ages have developed a colloquial language to talk about their craft. Fans have come up with some great names, including *washing machines, cheese slopes, MOC* ("my own creation"), *SNOT (studs not on top),* and of course *BURPs,* which stands for "big ugly rock pieces," which is a bit judgemental in my opinion, but hey, I'm not going to argue with the internet.

I'm a big advocate of these made-up names. The LEGO Group makes thousands of different brick shapes, and building a personal vocabulary helps you wrap your head around what pieces you have at your disposal. As you practice more and more, that personal vocabulary extends beyond individual part names and into techniques. There is a particular method of attaching arms to a figure's body I call "the Don Quixote shoulder" because, well . . . the first time I used it was on a model of Don Quixote. It's not super creative, but it works!

Coming up with your own names for your materials and techniques, no matter how silly it may feel, helps develop your creative process into something that is personal to you. Developing and advancing our creative language helps make vague and abstract ideas more concrete, which in turn makes it easier to understand those ideas. Emotions like joy and fear would exist without the words themselves but acknowledging something like fear by giving it a name makes it easier to *do something* about that fear. The same rings true for any creative pursuit—whether it's naming a new trick on a skateboard or describing a particular brush stroke while painting.

So go ahead and call that brick a "twofer;" it might just help make you a better builder.

. . . .

Build It:
Find the strangest looking piece in your collection. Give it
a unique name and build a model that makes it the star.

IN
SCALE

Think in Nanoscale

One of the questions that I'm asked most often is, "What's the biggest model you've ever made?" People are naturally drawn to things built at a grand scale, which makes sense, because it's very easy to see all the time and effort that goes into something like a 20-foot-tall LEGO® giraffe. To be honest, I'm always a bit uncomfortable answering the "biggest" question because the largest thing I've ever built (a full-size Christmas fireplace) isn't really that interesting. What I've found in my years as a Model Builder is that it's just as satisfying, if not more so, to scale down rather than up. My all-time favorite style of building, and one that's far, far easier to replicate at home, is nanoscale.

Nanoscale is the idea of trying to create something recognizable using as few elements as possible. I always liken it to the artistic concept of minimalism: reducing something down to its most essential elements. Oftentimes those "essential elements" are represented by simple shapes and color. A car becomes a rectangle atop two black circles. A house is nothing more than a white square with a triangle on top. One of my favorite examples is a duck built with three pieces: A yellow 1×2 brick for the body, an orange 1×2 plate for the beak, and a yellow 1×1 brick for the head.

Nanoscale building is about finding just the right brick for the job. The LEGO Group makes so many interesting and unique elements, which can be used in so many different ways, that finding *exactly* the right one might seem impossible. However, finding the right element isn't a problem if you work backward. I like to start by taking an unusual-looking element and inspecting it from all sides. Consider every little notch, curve, and angle of the brick. Does it have a hole that can represent an eye? Maybe a window? Is it curved in such a way to look like a shark's fin? Or the hood of a classic car?

If you've ever looked for shapes in clouds, this should all sound familiar. Interpreting something recognizable from abstract forms is a natural human impulse. Applying that impulse to nanoscale LEGO building is as relaxing as it is challenging and an excellent way to decompress with nothing more than a couple of bricks.

. . . .

Build It:
Build something using less than 10 bricks. Focus on color, shape, and purpose. Can you remove a brick and still express the same idea, even more simply?

915,
103,
765

WAYS

915,103,765 Ways

Here's a fun bit of LEGO® trivia: The number of configurations you can make with just six regular 2×4 bricks is an astronomical 915,103,756 unique combinations. If you put one together every five seconds it would take you 145 *years* of nonstop building to create every combination! The fact that 915,103,765 ways comes from an amount of bricks that can fit in the palm of your hand, well, it is wild to me.

When you start a creative project, there is so much potential in front of you, so many paths waiting to be explored. There are so many thoughts and ideas and emotions tucked into each step forward and each possible outcome. It's natural to want to attack from all directions, to try everything. But endless possibilities and also lead to lots of questions: "Maybe I should paint this instead of that? But would it be better if I did it this way? What color? What brush do I use? What style? Should this be a sculpture instead of a painting? Has that been done before?" These questions can be conscious or unconscious, but they can undermine your confidence. They can leave you chasing ten potential half-baked ideas just to try everything, instead of focusing in on one strong vision.

Seemingly limitless possibility can be overwhelming (it can make your eyes cross), but when you choose one direction and *commit*, the millions of "potential maybes" slip away. Sure, you may only end up with one way out of 9 million—and it may not even be *the best way* (if that exists!)—but in doing so, you're able to focus on pursuing a direction with purpose. A direction that is unique to you. Sometimes one way really is enough.

....

Build It:

Build a small model with six 2×4 bricks. Name it, photograph it, and claim it as your own. Pull up the photo when starting something new as a reminder that one way to the finish line is all that you need.

THE

OF

LANDSCAPING

The Joy of Landscaping

When building with LEGO® bricks, or creating anything, for that matter, it can be very easy to get distracted by focusing on the final product. You imagine winning the race while you're still running it. Scoring a goal before you kick. Getting married before you even ask someone on a first date. You lose sight of the joy of the moment, in favor of an imagined, superior end point down the road. While it's certainly important to keep your "eyes on the prize," as it were, there's also a unique joy to be found in building and creating with no end point in mind. This style of endless building is perfectly embodied in the idea of landscaping.

Landscapes and scenery are usually an afterthought to many builders—a background or accessories to give a model context and life. However, there is a simple kind of pleasure that comes from stacking dozens of gray slopes to make a rocky cliff face, or placing countless green plates to form the shape of a rolling hill. I think this joy comes from the fact that there's not really any clear "end point" when building something like a hill: It's an endlessly additive process. If you spend an hour making a hill, you have . . . a hill. If you spend TEN hours making a hill, you just have: *more hill*. One hundred hours? Just so, so much hill.

I realize I've said "hill" enough times now that it's starting to lose its meaning, and in a way that's also the idea behind endless building. The repetition of laying down brick after brick becomes a meditative process. Another great thing about the flow state—you're done when you want to be done and there's no wrong moves.

....

Build It:

Build a rainbow hill for as long as you'd like.

Small Parts

If you've built a LEGO® set in the past twenty years, you're likely familiar with the practice of numbering the bags that the bricks come in. *Wait! I know you're bored to tears already, but don't turn the page!* Yes, "bag numbering" is probably the least interesting aspect of any LEGO set, but hidden in those big bold 1s and 2s is an important lesson for tackling any project that seems too difficult.

It's easy to get overwhelmed when working on something large and complex. When you're building a set with thousands of pieces, you need to break it down into small parts first. Numbered bags divide the building process into smaller, manageable sections. As you complete them one by one, you feel a series of small accomplishments. The satisfaction that comes with these little victories help carry you through to your final goal: a finished model.

When designing your own LEGO creations, those goals become a little more abstract. Without the reassuring crinkle of "bag 7" being thrown aside, we're left having to decide what our incremental goals will be. One strategy that I will often use when designing a complex model is to break it down on paper first. Take the example of a pirate ship. To finish that model, I'll need to build a mast, sails, and a crow's nest. The main body of the ship might seem daunting, but I can break it up further by creating individual designs for a porthole window, a side railing, a rudder, and a figurehead. Of course we want to bring our scene to life, so add to the list some ocean waves on a blue baseplate, a healthy supply of pirate minifigures, and a couple (dozen) crates of rum bottles.

In breaking down the model this way, you're essentially making a checklist titled "Things to Build." With each item that gets crossed off the list, take a small moment to appreciate all that you've done so far. Let each little victory carry you through to the next, and in doing so you'll make quick work of even the most complex challenges.

....

Build It:

Dream up a LEGO model that seems "out of reach," something that seems too big, too complex, or too *something*. Choose one small, seemingly insignificant detail of that idea to build. Label it "Step 1."

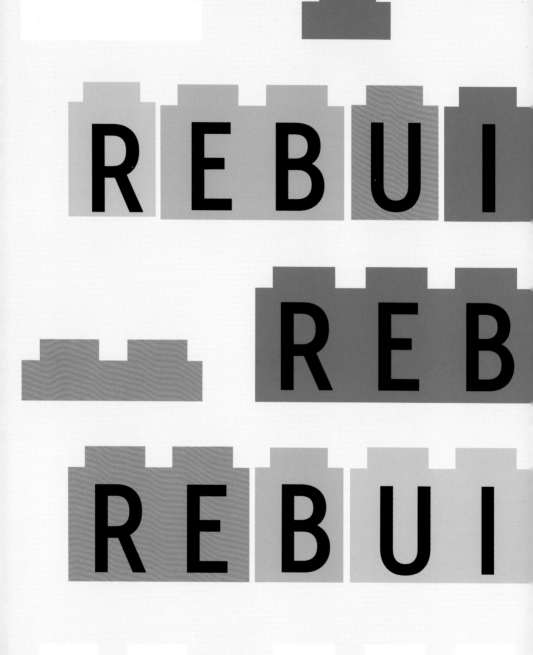

REBUI

REB

REBUI

AND   REBUILD

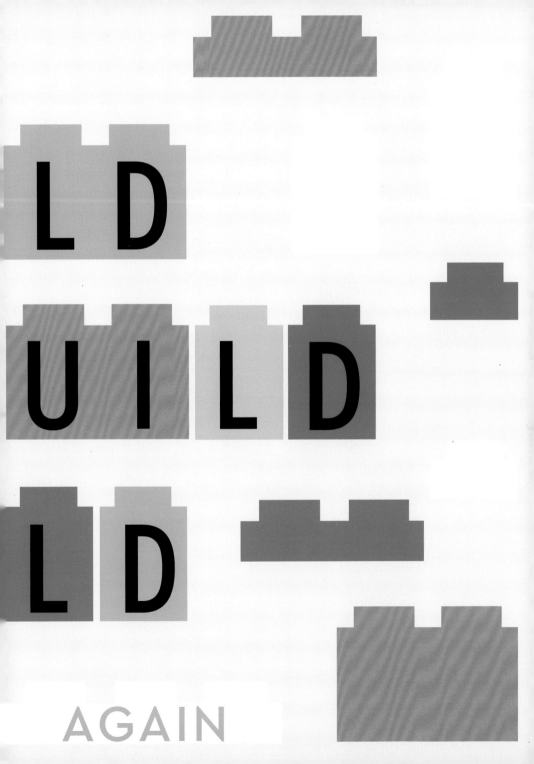

LD
UILD
LD

AGAIN

9

Rebuild, Rebuild, Rebuild, and Rebuild Again

If there's one thing that *every* LEGOLAND Model Builder knows how to make, it's "minilanders." Boy, oh boy do you have to build a *ton* of minilanders. A minilander is basically a brick-built LEGO® person. Their bodies are nothing more than a few 2×4s stacked up with a single brick for a head and a couple of plates for the hair. Hinged plates make up their arms, and tall, inverted slopes are the usual way to make the legs. There are *hundreds* of these figures populating the Miniland LEGO® City at each LEGOLAND theme park.

In building these figures over and over again, you start to see where little changes can be made to give each person their own distinct character. Using clips instead of plates gives the hair more texture. Swapping out a 2×4 for a 2×3 gives the minilander a smaller waist. Adding a slight angle at the hip and placing one hand there gives the little guy a whole lot of sass. By repeatedly creating the same thing again and again, you start to develop a mastery over it. This mastery gives you a comfortable home base from which you can branch out to explore new styles and techniques. By having a tried-and-true method to fall back on, you're giving yourself a creative safety net that makes it easier to take the risks needed to advance and grow.

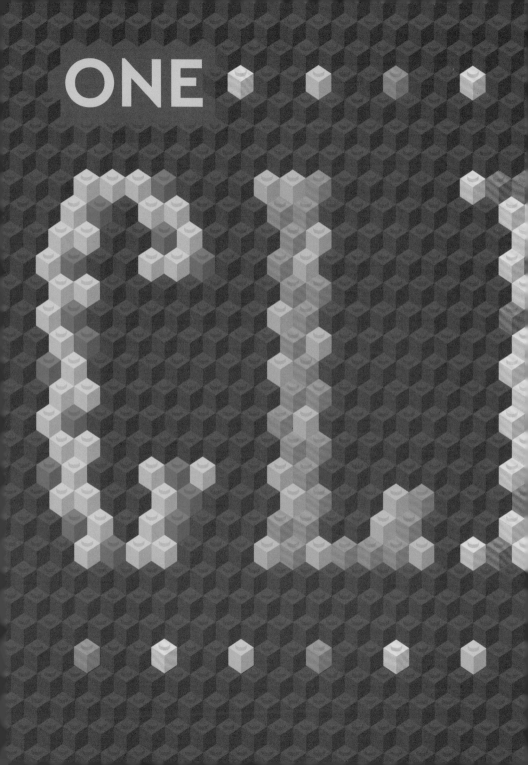

ONE

01.

ONE BRICK AT A TIME

One Click at a Time

For a lot of people, making the leap from building with instructions to designing on your own can seem impossible. It can be overwhelming to create anything from scratch. It's like cooking or baking—how do you make the leap from a familiar method to your own secret recipe? Where do you even begin? Well, by not throwing out a perfectly good cookbook!

When venturing out on your own, it helps to start from a solid, trusted foundation. Even though it seems counterintuitive, give yourself boundaries to be creative within. While rules are often perceived as restrictive in some way, they can also help narrow in on a vision more quickly. An excellent first step to go from set builder to MOC designer is to build within the guidelines of a preexisting set. Take something you've built with instructions and remix it to make it your own.

The changes you make at first don't have to be radical. They can be as simple as rearranging the pedals on a LEGO® flower or changing the pattern of the roof tiles for a building. The goal in making these changes is to become comfortable making your own aesthetic choices for designs. Assess the model after you've made the change. Does it look better? Worse? Keep reworking it until you find something you're happy with. As you get into the rhythm of making these changes, allow yourself to take apart more and more of the model. Don't worry about not being able to put it back together "correctly"; you're making it your own and, after all, you always have the instructions to fall back on.

Building your own models starts one click at a time. Adding and subtracting is like finding your own balance of salt or adjusting the spice on your favorite dish. Small changes lead to big ones, and when you start from a strong place (like an already-designed LEGO set) you're giving yourself a solid foundation from which you can grow.

. . . .

Build It:

Find a set that's been gathering dust on a shelf. Take it apart, by repositioning one brick at a time. Try to make something original, gradually, using only those elements.

BUILD

DUCK

Build a Duck

It was strange when I got my job as a Model Builder at LEGOLAND®
Arizona. I didn't really *feel* like a professional anything. My job title
was so lofty, and had so much implied expectation, that I didn't
really feel like I could live up to it. For the first year, my perceived
skill level and my title felt disjointed to me, and I suffered from a
healthy dose of imposter syndrome. I found myself frequently comparing my own work to the work of others, and I was often embar-
rassed to display things I built. It was hard to find the joy in building
when I spent all day questioning my own skills.

What ultimately broke me out of this cycle was a mantra I'd repeat
whenever I'd feel myself slipping back into that self-critical style of
thinking: "It doesn't have to be perfect." When it comes to building
with LEGO® bricks, there is *no such thing* as perfect. In a system of
endless possibilities and combinations, perfection doesn't exist. Let
that sink in for a minute!

People have a tendency to hyper-focus on the flaws in something,
especially something they themselves have created. In acknowledging and accepting that those flaws are going to be there no
matter what, it becomes easier to look at the big picture. When

you step back and breathe, you're able to see your successes alongside your shortcomings. You don't have to be ecstatic with what you've made (or even happy at all, for that matter), but what you should do is realize that it has value, even if it's just a stepping-stone to something you create in the future.

There is a famous activity that the LEGO Group asks new hires to complete at the beginning of their training. They offer everyone in the room the same set of bricks, set a timer, and give a simple instruction: Please build a duck. (One of the first LEGO toys ever built was a wooden duck, so it's a nice callback to the company's roots.) Everyone scrambles to assemble the core parts: head, bill, body, legs before the building time is over. The room is suddenly filled with ducks—tall ones, square ones, flat ones, one-legged ones—ducks of all shapes and sizes. And guess what? In the end, they're all ducks. In the LEGO system, there is no "right way" to build a duck. There is only *your* way.

Allow yourself to create without expectation. It's okay if you think your design could be better: The work you put into creating something "bad" feeds into making you a stronger designer, artist, engineer, or whatever it is you're interested in achieving. Reminding yourself of this every day is your best line of defense in maintaining a growth mindset and progressing as an artist.

....

Build It:

Build a duck using six LEGO bricks in just 3 minutes. When you're done, take a moment to appreciate your successes while acknowledging where there is room for improvement. Unbuild it and find another way to express a duck using the same bricks.

FLIP

UP4

DOU

12

Flip It
Upside Down

Hiding in the underside of one of my favorite elements (part no. 26047 for you super nerds) is a happy little face. This, of course, is entirely unintentional. The brick I'm talking about is basically a single rounded stud with a small horizontal bar attached to one end. The hole in the bottom (or to use the technical term, *antistud*) is rounded on one side and squared off on the other. Just above this antistud, on the plastic where the horizontal bar attaches, are two tiny, tiny holes. These holes are nothing more than a side effect of the manufacturing process, however, when looked at in tandem with that half-rounded antistud, it's hard not to see two eyes and a wide, grinning mouth.

I've since built an army of super tiny, super happy snails using that piece: I give them out to guests who visit me at LEGOLAND® Arizona and use them to teach the concept of negative space. What's crazy is that I had used that brick in dozens of builds before I stumbled on the little secret hiding on the underside. It was there all along, but it wasn't until I considered the piece from a new perspective that I was able to see it.

In working through any creative challenge, you're going to, inevitably, hit a wall. One way to break through is to change your perspective. Approach the problem from another angle. Write a song backward, starting from an awesome last line. Sketch from the feet up. Flip the bridge you're building and turn it into an even cooler tunnel. Instead of waiting for the solution to just reveal itself, actively change your viewpoint. You might just find a smile hiding where you'd never expect to see one.

. . . .

Build It:

Take the largest LEGO® plate you own and flip it upside down. Use this as the base of a model, and take note of how building upside down forces you to think about the pieces differently.

BACK THE

TO
BIN

Back to the Bin

Failure is the most important part of success, but it still sounds like a dirty word. *Failure.* You have FAILED. You did it wrong and everything is terrible. Pack it up, you're done. These are easy things to tell yourself when something doesn't work out, but the thing is, they're just not true. You haven't failed: You've just learned what doesn't work.

There inevitably comes a time when building a model where you look at it and just say, *No, this is just . . . this is bad . . . what have I done?* But that doesn't mean that the mess of a MOC you're looking at doesn't have value. Take a closer look at it from all sides. There are likely aspects of it that look decent, maybe even good! Even if they're totally overshadowed by what *didn't* work, those little bits that you like can be repurposed back into a new design. If you spend two hours trying to build a majestic lion only for it to look like a tired dog, you haven't failed or wasted your time, you're just two hours closer to a finished model. It's okay to admit when you're done with one direction. Just go back to the LEGO® bin and try another way. When you start over fresh, you'll be better equipped to find the right path to the masterpiece in your head.

I should point out that this is a bit of a "rinse and repeat" process. In my own experience as a Model Builder, I will restart a model an average of three or four times before I find a route that I feel comfortable pursuing to an end. It's easy to get discouraged on that second or third rebuild, but what I've found that helps is to document the process. Take pictures of your "failed attempts" before you break them down and start over. The utility here is twofold: (1) You have reference images to help stop you from making the same mistakes twice, and (2) once you finish your model, you'll be able to see the improvements that were made from starting over. Embracing, and even celebrating, your failures will help make you a better builder.

· ·

Build It:

Take a photo of a "failed" attempt at a LEGO creation. Keep working on that build until you're happy with how it looks, then display both the finished product and the work in progress photo in your work area to remind yourself that failure is just part of the process.

Find the
Hidden Hack

Making a circle out of squares is one of the harder things you can do with LEGO® bricks. Turning that circle into a three-dimensional sphere is another challenge altogether. In fact, one of the first tests given to newly hired model builders at the LEGOLAND® model shop is to create a perfect sphere that will survive a two-story drop. Now if building a sphere sounds too daunting for you to try, don't worry—there *is* a trick to it.

The thing about a sphere is that, by definition, it's the same on all sides. That means that if you design just the top half of the sphere, you can copy it brick for brick on the bottom. What's more: Those halves can be broken into quadrants, like four big slices of a colorful, plastic pie (please do not eat the LEGO bricks). If you design just one of these slices, that same shape can be copied for the other three. In the end you really have to design only one-eighth of a sphere. It's still a challenging build no matter how you slice it (sorry), but it's much more manageable when you break it down this way.

Little shortcuts (or "hacks," if you want to think in internet click-bait terms) like these are hiding in everything you do. Taking time at the start of a project to look for them can save you hours of stress in the long run. Don't confuse "the hard way" of doing things with "the best way": Making things easier on yourself isn't cheating. If you've ever watched the painter Bob Ross work, you know he doesn't paint every single leaf on every single tree; he creates whole forests with just a couple of squiggly brush strokes. If anyone ever calls you out for doing something the easy way (first off, they're wrong), tell them you're doing it like Bob Ross would.

Build It:

Lay down an 8×8 plate. Add a 1×6 plate to each side to make it appear "rounder." Make this shape 5 plates thick: This is the very center of your sphere. Try to create a ball, remembering that you need to design only one-eighth of it.

TAKE

IN VE

NTORY

15

Take Inventory

There are two prevailing theories about how to approach building LEGO® sets. There are builders who just dump the pieces on the table and start, and there are those who meticulously sort their parts by color or shape to set up a well-organized workspace. I was originally in the "comfort in clutter" camp, but over the years I've started shifting toward a more organized approach. As my LEGO building workshop has grown to include more and more elements, I've found myself enjoying the quiet meditation that comes with organizing my collection and taking stock of what's in front of me. While it always tempting to order a new set, or spend a day at the pick-a-brick getting exactly the parts you think you need, I think it's just as important to take a moment to inventory what you already have.

We use hobbies to relax and unwind from the stress of the "real world." Sometimes, though, our hobbies can feel just as demanding. Cleaning old paint from your brushes. Restringing a guitar. Chopping all the ingredients for a recipe. Organizing your LEGO bricks. These are activities secondary to our main hobby, but they serve an important purpose. If we're able to find pleasure in these small asides, then it only goes to bolster our love for that hobby. Let these upkeep moments become little rituals. Use them to reflect on how far you've come in developing your skills as a builder. Think about where you'd like to go next, what else you'd like to achieve. In taking the time to take stock you might even find something you didn't know you had.

. . . .

Build It:

Take part of your collection and lay it out on a table so that you can see everything. Sort by color and shape. Try to find some bricks and parts of sets that you had forgotten about and take the time to rediscover them.

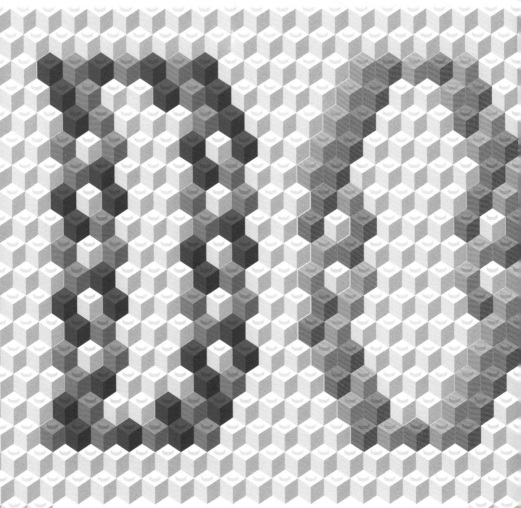

CONNECT THE

(AND TILES,

AND PLATES)

16

Connect the Dots (and Tiles, and Plates)

When you think of LEGO® bricks, your mind probably goes to traditional sets. Skyscrapers, spaceships, or robots with fleshed-out interiors rendered beautifully in three dimensions. Just as satisfying, though, can be using LEGO elements to create two-dimensional mosaic art. Using nothing but flat plates, dots, and tiles, you can create vibrant and impressive works of art that invoke the spirit of pop artists like Andy Warhol or scaled-back "pixel" art inspired by classic video games.

When you're building in two dimensions rather than three, you have to take more care in considering perspective. If your subject is something that exists in three-dimensional space, aspects of it will seem warped. Things coming toward you will seem smaller or strangely angled. Anything perpendicular to your vision might seem too large. It's important to allow your brain to "flatten" what you see into two dimensions. You need to train yourself to take what you see at face value, and build what's in front of you, rather than what you imagine it to look like in your head.

Let's say you're trying to design a mosaic of an airplane taking off. You choose to interpret it from a profile, such that you see the plane from the side with a sunset in the background. From this perspective you have one wing coming toward you and one wing pointed directly away. The wing that's facing away from you is going to be mostly obscured: You're going to be able to see only a small bit of it poking out from the body of the plane. Your brain is going to come in, being all smart as it is, and say, *There's a wing there! I know it! Planes have two wings! Add a wing to that side of your mosaic right now!* You have to fight the temptation. *Yes, brain, planes do have two wings; you're very smart and I'm very proud of you, but that's not how it looks from* this angle. There might be some pushback at first, but when you allow yourself to see things as they are before you, and push your biases aside, you become more effective at understanding and interpreting your surroundings. It's important not to confuse how you imagine something to be with how it actually is.

. . . .

Build It:

Set up a still-life scene using objects from around your house. Build a mosaic portrait of the scene on a 32×32 baseplate, trying to interpret what you see as flat shapes and colors rather than three-dimensional objects.

STA
AT

Start at 1×1

LEGO® models have come a long way over the years. The LEGO Group was founded in Billund, Denmark, in 1932. The bricks we'd recognize today (those made with ABS plastic) were first released in 1964. Since then, we've seen the introduction of now-iconic staples of LEGO sets like minifigures and the LEGO® Technic building system, as well as the occasional strange but charming hiccup (I'm looking at you, Galidor . . .).

With this continual innovation and advancement, we've also seen a serious uptick in the *difficulty* of some LEGO sets. Thousands of available parts, combined with the serious talent of the LEGO team of designers, has led to a vast library of advanced techniques, styles, and tricks that make modern sets as incredible as they are challenging. However, just because all these crazy new techniques exist doesn't mean we should discount what made LEGO bricks so awesome back in the 1960s. Making a simple tower out of a couple of basic bricks can be just as rewarding as creating a working pop-up book if you allow yourself to take on a beginner's mindset.

To the beginner, everything is new and filled with possibilities. Any new technique you learn and any new piece you acquire opens up whole new worlds of creation. As you advance as a builder, and your repertoire grows, it's easy to lose that sense of wonder. When you feel like you've seen it all, it becomes very hard to be impressed by anything.

Fortunately, though, it doesn't have to be that way. That dismissive attitude is a choice. It's a choice that makes it harder to enjoy doing the things that you love, and one that gets in the way of progressing past a certain point. Allowing yourself to open up and appreciate what's basic and what's easy will enrich your experiences. When you take time to enjoy the simple alongside the advanced, all you're doing is giving yourself more to enjoy.

. . . .

Build It:

Design something using only your collection of 1×1 bricks.

18

Nice Part Usage

In my first year working as a Model Builder, I had a stubborn habit. Whenever I was designing something, I made it a point to not look up other MOCs similar to what I was creating. I had this weird notion that seeing how others built things would "taint" my own vision, or that it was in some way cheating. The best thing I've done for myself in all my years of LEGO® building is realizing that this way of thinking is just plain dumb. The talented and elusive street artist Banksy once said, "Good artists imitate, great artists steal," a quote he took from Picasso.

Now I'm not suggesting you take someone else's designs to sell on the internet for profit. That's bad. Please don't do that. What I am saying is that even if you borrow ideas wholesale from existing sets, your own ideas and style are inevitably going to seep into the build and make it your own. In LEGO lingo there is a term, *NPU*, or "nice part usage." It's a way to say: *Hey, fellow builder, I see what you're doing there, and it's awesome and exciting.* LEGO elements can each be used in countless ways, so giving someone an NPU shout-out is all about encouraging their creativity and building a bond around thinking outside the grid.

Art, design, and engineering are collective in nature, and each new thing builds on the last. So instead of pretending you're in it alone, why not throw a fellow builder an *NPU* and see if they've come up with a solution that could help your own work.

If you could build (out of LEGO bricks, of course) a telescope that let you see into the past, and you pointed it at whichever crazy-complicated, expert-level set released this year, you'd see a long line of designers and builders stretching back all the way to 1954 when the first LEGO set was released, and each one of them would be looking over their shoulder to borrow the best ideas from the person who came before them.

And if you *do* build this reality-defying LEGO telescope, please, *please* post a picture of it online so I can steal your design.

. . . .

Build It:

Take some existing element from a LEGO set—a functional LEGO® Technic mechanism, the roof of a modular, the chassis of a car—and use this as a foundation for your own design.

EMBR

BLUE

19

Embrace the Blue

Part of what makes building a LEGO® set an enjoyable way to unwind is that you're given such clear direction. There's no question about where to begin: You crack open the instructions and look to step one. As your building abilities grow, there may come a time when you want to make the transition from expert set builder to budding MOC designer. That means doing away with the clear one-step-at-a-time style of building in favor of the exciting and daunting world of pure imagination (cue the Willy Wonka music!). While you will certainly run into countless challenges of *how* to create your own designs, a hurdle that is often overlooked, and one that you will encounter before any questions of "how," is coming up with *what* to build. Coming up with good ideas can be a challenge. You can build *literally anything* with LEGO bricks, and that freedom can be overwhelming.

An effective method for overcoming idea paralysis is the concept of blue sky thinking. With blue sky thinking, there are no bad ideas. Everything is valid, and nothing is "too big" or "too complex" to be considered. Thinking without limits allows your brain to barrel forward unimpeded, causing ideas to lead to other ideas. Bad ideas can spark good ones. Something impossibly grand and elaborate can be the inspirational foundation for something just as awesome but far more grounded. A lot of the time the hardest part of creating is getting started and gathering momentum. By allowing yourself to dream stuff up without the expectation of having to follow through, you're getting into a creative groove and those realistic (but still awesome!) ideas will start to flow.

. . . .

Build It:
What would you build if you had unlimited bricks
and unlimited time? Use your answer as inspiration for
a smaller build. Create a microscale version of it, or
attempt to design one detail from your grand vision.

BREAKING

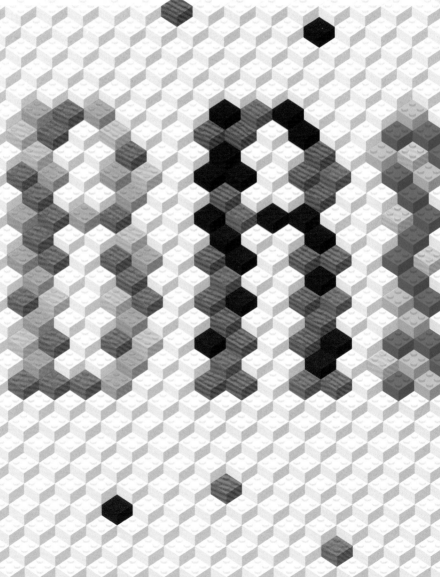

BACK TO

Breaking
Back to Bricks

In my job as Model Builder, I end up getting asked the same questions over and over again. One of the most frequent is, "How mad would you be if this or that model broke?" The truth is, while I never *like* seeing my creations destroyed, you learn very quickly not to get too precious about keeping models together. The destructive capabilities of small children in large groups is really something to behold, and even the most expertly designed, well-glued model is bound to break at some point. I've seen skyscrapers torn from build tables and whole shelves of models fall from the wall. Broken builds are just part of playing with LEGO® bricks, and I think they should be seen as an opportunity rather than a tragedy.

That initial crash of plastic on the floor may hurt at first. Give yourself a moment to mourn, but don't dwell on it too long before considering your options. You can rebuild the set, letting yourself revisit the experience that initially made you want to buy the model in the first place. Even if you tossed or lost the instructions, the LEGO Group makes all their building instructions available online, meaning no set is ever broken for good. Alternatively: Take this as an opportunity to try designing a MOC. If building without instructions is something you've always wanted to try but never found the time for, take this as a sign. The beauty about LEGO building is that LEGO sets never really break; they just become loose brick.

....

Build It:

Build a model that's meant to be broken.
Design something that smashes in a spectacular way.
Drop it, and let the catharsis wash over you.

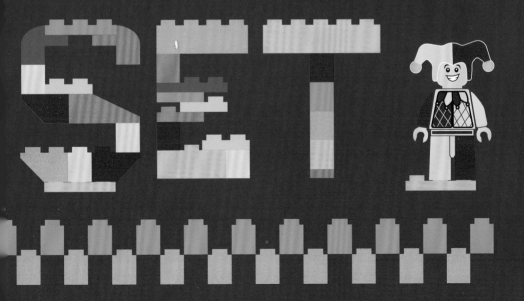

FIGURE
SET

21 Minifigure Mindset

The original minifigure, released in 1978, had a distinctive expression—a warm, knowing smile fans lovingly refer to as "two dots and a line." The minifigure expression has become iconic—known around the world as a symbol of creativity, play, and pure imagination. The minifigure represents all of us, and all the possibilities of the world we live in. And, man, is that original minifigure was just happy to be here. From outer space exploration to delivering the mail in LEGO® City, the minifigure's joy is palpable and pure. You can't help but smile at that smile.

When I'm in a tough place at work or in other parts of my life, stuck on a project or feeling uninspired, I sometimes try to find my own minifigure mindset. Now, don't get me wrong, I'm not saying you need to just grin your way through your problems; that's not healthy either. But I think that minifigures can also remind us to practice daily gratitude—to find even just a sliver of good in the hardest of times. Embracing a minifigure mindset helps me remember to stop, pause, and reflect every day— something that makes me a better builder and human being.

Build It:

Build yourself a home. I know, I know, it sounds a little silly at first. No one is watching, so just go for it. Populate this ideal living space with minifigures that represent people from your life. Who would be there? What would you say that you've been meaning to say? Use this simple prompt as a moment to reflect on and celebrate the relationships you value.

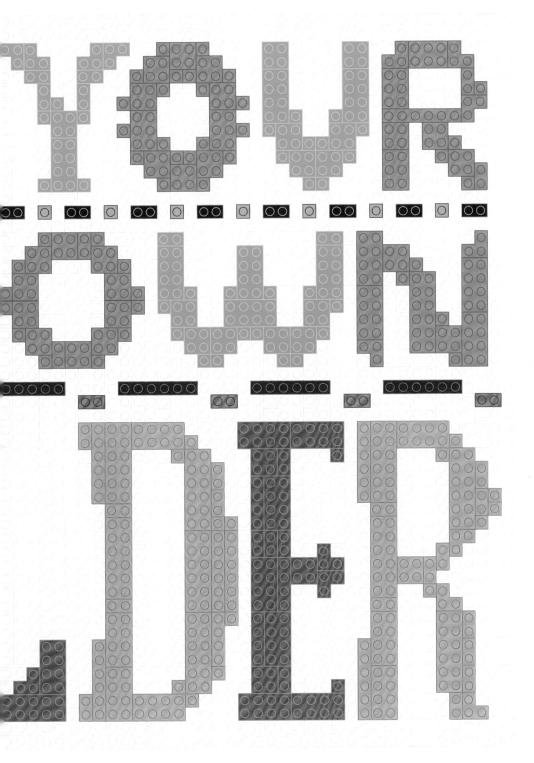

Be Your
Own Builder

Just be yourself is my least favorite advice. It's generic, it's unhelpful, it's so broad, and it's the first phrase people seem to latch on to when dishing out tips on how to be more creative. It's hard *not* to be yourself. By definition anything you do is . . . well . . . you doing it. But I get the sentiment behind it, so in response to this, my least favorite advice, I offer an equally generic (but hopefully more directed) platitude: *Do it for you.* Whatever it is you're doing, do it how you want to, and for your own reasons.

Your own happiness and self-worth should come first in your hobbies and art. As with any medium, there are so many different ways to engage with the LEGO® system. Minifigure photography, mosaic building, designing MOCs, and the joy of just *collecting* every set of a certain LEGO series are all perfectly valid ways to derive enjoyment from the hobby. *Anything* you do is going to be more rewarding, more validating, and just plain better if you're doing it on your own terms, in the way you want to.

Looking to other people's work for inspiration is great, but when you start comparing your own work to theirs, or start imitating what they do because you feel like it's "better," all you're doing is muddying your creativity and making things harder for yourself in the long run. Don't be afraid of your own instincts: Embrace them and let your own voice shine through in everything you do.

....

Build It:
Be your own model. Build a minifigure
of yourself to add to your favorite set.

About the Author

Alec Posta lives and builds in Phoenix, Arizona. In 2016, Posta won the Brick Factor competition to become the Model Builder at LEGOLAND® Discovery Center Arizona. Posta designs and builds custom LEGO models, as well as develops classes, events, and activities for guests with an emphasis on learning through play. Besides building, Posta enjoys making music, cooking, and playing board games with his wife, Becky, and their friends.